SERIES 235

In this book, we will look at the movement of
people after the Second World War and
explore the significance of the arrival of
HMT *Empire Windrush* to England in 1948.

LADYBIRD BOOKS

UK | USA | Canada | Ireland | Australia
India | New Zealand | South Africa

Ladybird Books is part of the Penguin Random House group of companies
whose addresses can be found at global.penguinrandomhouse.com.

www.penguin.co.uk   www.puffin.co.uk   www.ladybird.co.uk

First published 2023
001

Printed in China

The authorized representative in the EEA is Penguin Random House Ireland,
Morrison Chambers, 32 Nassau Street, Dublin D02 YH68

A CIP catalogue record for this book is available from the British Library
ISBN: 978-0-241-54420-4
All correspondence to:
Ladybird Books
Penguin Random House Children's
One Embassy Gardens, 8 Viaduct Gardens
London SW11 7BW

MIX
Paper from
responsible sources
FSC
www.fsc.org   FSC® C018179

Windrush

A Ladybird Book

Written by Colin Grant and Emma Dyer

Illustrated by Melleny Taylor

Colonial rule

Around 400 years ago, Britain claimed that some of the islands in the Caribbean belonged to them and, despite being nearly 5,000 miles (8,047 km) away, the British called these islands British "colonies". They wanted to use the land to grow crops such as sugar and tobacco to make Britain rich. At the time, Britain claimed colonies all over the world, and together these were known as the "British Empire".

For hundreds of years, the British Empire controlled the Caribbean, or "West Indies" as they were known. The British would bring owned, or enslaved, people from Africa to the Caribbean and made them work in the fields, which they called "plantations". Slavery is the theft of people: forcing them to work without pay and with punishments, including death, if they resist. British people bought and sold enslaved people as easily as they traded goods and materials.

Until 1833, many British people accepted slavery as part of British life. But rebellions on all the islands of the Caribbean – and the fear of enslaved people fighting for their freedom – eventually brought about change and the end of slavery. Britain still had its colonies, but people were now paid for their work. History often commemorates the people who were against slavery more readily than the enslaved people themselves, but a statue of Bussa – an enslaved rebel leader – stands in Barbados today to celebrate the freedom of the oppressed.

Part of the Empire

As well as enslaved people, Britain also sent British people to the Caribbean. This was to make sure that the Empire remained under British control, to ensure that the islands were working hard and to see that any profit made in the Caribbean would be sent back to Britain. The presence of British people on the islands also meant that British culture and customs were introduced and then enforced and upheld.

Surrounded by British influence, people in the West Indies soon began to feel like they were a part of a wider British culture. Britain became known as the "motherland", and if anyone wanted to travel outside of the Caribbean islands, they would apply for and be given a British passport because they were British citizens. Britain provided the West Indies with goods and services, and some West Indian people were proud to think of themselves as British.

From the first celebrations in 1902, and for years afterwards, children living in British colonies around the world would celebrate "Empire Day" by waving Union Jack flags and singing songs. They would stand together in school playgrounds in a big circle and join hands – an act meant to persuade children that they were part of one big "family", the British Empire. Not everyone was happy about the Empire Day celebrations. Many West Indians felt that they should not be celebrating a country that had brought slavery to their shores and treated them so badly.

War is coming

When the First World War began in 1914, it was not just British people who volunteered to fight for Britain. The wide reach of the Empire and its influence meant that other non-European countries sent money as well as soldiers to fight in the British war effort. In 1915, the British West Indies Regiment (BWIR) was formed as a separate unit within the British Army. By the end of the war in 1918, there were twelve BWIR battalions made up of volunteer soldiers from British Guiana and all the Caribbean colonies.

At the end of the First World War, some soldiers from British colonies, as well as West Indian men who worked on merchant ships, delivering steel, coal and different kinds of foods, decided to stay and bring up families in Britain. To them, they were "coming home" to live in and be part of greater Britain. For example, many people from the Caribbean who settled in Britain were musicians and singers. The West Indian Dance Orchestra became the leading swing band in Britain and was famous as the all-Black orchestra that played jazz at the Café de Paris in London.

However, in 1939, the country was shaken by the outbreak of war again. Britain had still not recovered from the death and destruction caused by the First World War, and so the call-to-arms was loud and spread far and wide – with civilians, settlers and the wider British colonies being asked to fight on the side of Britain once more.

Answering the call

At the start of the Second World War in 1939, West Indians living in the Caribbean were asked by the British government to join the British army, navy or air force and fight under the British flag as part of the Allied forces. Ten thousand West Indian men and women proudly signed up, cheered on by family and friends. Quite a few volunteers had relatives who had fought and died for Britain in the First World War, and they saw this call-to-arms as not only an adventure or a duty, but also the chance to carry on the tradition of service.

This loyalty to Britain was a result of being under Empire control, and part of West Indian life at the time. People would often hang paintings of famous British buildings on their walls and there would usually be a portrait of the King of England in the house. In cinemas, before the film began, people would stand up to sing the British national anthem. Schools taught from British books, such as *Nelson's West Indian Readers*, and children would learn traditional British country dances and famous British poems by heart.

The West Indian soldiers who answered the call had to travel to Britain to complete their training before being sent to fight in mainland Europe. Other volunteers were sent to work in factories to make guns and bullets and to build ships for the war. Those volunteers who missed their families in the Caribbean kept in touch by writing letters and through BBC radio programmes broadcast from London.

The Nationality Act of 1948

The Second World War lasted six years, from 1939 to 1945, and it involved the majority of the world's countries. When the war came to an end, a period of recovery began and people started to look for new opportunities and began to move – or "migrate" – to other countries. Hundreds of thousands of British people left to find work in New Zealand, Australia and Canada, and ships such as the SS *Ormonde* and SS *Almanzora* brought people to Britain, too. Passengers included both civilians in search of work and soldiers from other countries returning to rejoin the British military.

The result of a devastating war and the new mass movement of people created a shortfall of workers in Britain, and so the British Nationality Act was introduced in 1948. This act offered British citizenship to any person born in the United Kingdom or its colonies and invited people to come and join the effort to rebuild the nation. It also reminded Britons that people from the colonies were not only needed to help to do important work, but that they had a right to be in Britain, too.

The price of tickets to Britain from the West Indies was supposed to be cheap enough to encourage young people to travel. But tickets were still very expensive, and often families did not have enough money to travel together, so just one person was sent on ahead. Farmers were even known to sell half of their livestock just to buy a single ticket.

HMT *Empire Windrush*

His Majesty's Troopship (HMT) *Empire Windrush* was built
in Germany, under the name *Monte Rosa*. It was originally
a German ship, but by the end of the Second World War,
it had been claimed by the British and renamed *Windrush*
after the river in Gloucestershire. In 1948, HMT *Empire
Windrush* became a significant ship by being the first major
passenger ship to arrive in Britain after the Nationality Act
had been passed.

In May 1948, HMT *Empire Windrush* was travelling from
Australia to England via the West Indies to pick up
servicemen who were on leave. The first passengers who
boarded were from Trinidad, then the ship sailed on to dock
in Kingston, Jamaica, but it became clear the ship would not
be full. Seizing the opportunity, the ship's owners placed
adverts in Caribbean newspapers offering tickets to citizens.
These adverts were met with a lot of excitement, especially
because they gave people the chance to go to Britain.

The price for a one-way ticket was £28 and 10 shillings,
which is equivalent to about £1,000 today. This "special
price" was still very expensive, and only about a quarter of
the people who wanted a ticket were able to go. People
coming from the Caribbean were also encouraged to bring
letters from trusted people to vouch that they were hard
workers of good character, in order to help them find a
place to live and work in Britain.

Life on board

When HMT *Empire Windrush* left the Jamaican docks, it travelled to Tampico, Mexico, Havana, Cuba and Bermuda before heading to Britain. By the time it reached the open waters of the Atlantic Ocean, the ship had 1,027 passengers on board, including people from Poland, Mexico, Britain, the Caribbean, Myanmar and Gibraltar. Official ship records state that 802 passengers gave their last country of residence as somewhere in the Caribbean, with 539 of those people being residents of Jamaica. There were 684 men, 257 women and 86 children on board, and the average age of the passengers was 24 years old.

As well as a sense of adventure, passengers had another thing in common: a sense of style! People dressed up in their most stylish clothes, even though the British government had told them that the ship was quite dirty. Flowery dresses and "zoot suits", an oversized style of suit that was fashionable at the time, were on display alongside military uniforms.

The ship became home to several stowaways – people travelling without a ticket. The captain announced that if a passenger was not able to produce their ticket when asked, they would be forcibly sent home and potentially put in prison. To help them, some of the West Indian musicians put on a concert to raise money. The famous jazz singer Mona Baptiste sang, and enough money was raised to buy the stowaways their tickets and save them from prison.

Arriving at Tilbury Docks, Essex

It would take HMT *Empire Windrush* around three weeks to cross the Atlantic and arrive in Britain. There was an electric atmosphere on the ship, particularly when the famous White Cliffs of Dover came into view. The ship finally arrived at Tilbury Docks, Essex on 22 June 1948. Passengers looked smart as they disembarked. There was no tradition of wearing fedora hats at home in the Caribbean, but many passengers had bought them specially for the occasion.

One of the passengers was Aldwyn Roberts, the calypsonian who took the stage name of Lord Kitchener. He wrote the famous song "London is the Place for Me". He sang it on arrival, and reporters at the docks thought he had made it up on the spot, but actually it was a "song of the journey", as Aldwyn had started writing it when he left Trinidad.

The arrival of HMT *Empire Windrush* was turned into a significant event by the media. Cameras and news reporters had not been sent to record any of the previous ships arriving from the Caribbean, such as the SS *Ormonde* in 1947, or to meet the planes arriving with people. Media attention was given to the arrival of HMT *Empire Windrush* because it landed in Britain in the same year that the Nationality Act was signed. This gave rise to the false idea that HMT *Empire Windrush* was the first ship when, in fact, it was one of many.

Coming "home"

Most of the HMT *Empire Windrush* passengers planned to settle in London on arrival, although a number had arranged to travel on to other cities, such as Liverpool, Birmingham and Bristol.

While some new arrivals remember a friendly welcome, many were shocked by how badly they were treated. One British broadcaster (the BBC) had made a booklet called "Going to Britain?" to give people an idea of what to expect. It contained tips such as how to queue in shops and how to talk to strangers in the street, but it did not prepare people for how difficult it would be to find somewhere to live.

Many British landlords did not want Black people staying in their houses, and even the famous West Indian cricketer Learie Constantine was told that he would not be allowed to stay in a hotel with his family. It became such a common experience that some people from the Caribbean would let the landlord know in advance that they were Black so that they would not waste their time going to see somewhere, only to be turned away because of the colour of their skin.

Racial discrimination and prejudice were allowed to flourish, and it became more visible as racist signs appeared in windows of boarding houses, actively turning Black people away. This attitude forced some people to sleep on the streets because there was nowhere else to go.

Finding work

Despite being invited to come and work by the British government, West Indian workers were often turned away when they looked for a job. Some were told that the job had already gone, even if that was not true, and some saw factory owners hang racist signs on their gates, saying "No coloureds". People from the Caribbean were hurt by how badly they were treated, but mostly they would walk away with the resolve to try to find a job elsewhere. They needed money to survive, and work was the only option.

Many of these jobseekers were skilled workers, such as clerks, tailors, cabinet makers and scholars. They had received a good, "British" education in their colonial schools and expected a warm welcome and huge opportunities on arrival in the "motherland". But in reality, they were often only offered the more menial, dirty or dangerous jobs, including building work, street sweeping, cleaning or working in coal mines.

However, some British establishments began to deliberately recruit people from the West Indies. The National Health Service, which was set up in 1948, became a large recruiter, with jobs available in hospital administration, cleaning and nursing. The railway companies accepted all workers and, in the late 1950s, London Transport even set up offices in the West Indies to offer jobs on London buses to people who wanted to live and work in Britain.

Settling in

West Indians had been given a very romantic idea of Britain, thanks to the books they read and the films they watched when they were growing up. After arriving in Britain, they would visit famous landmarks such as Trafalgar Square or Piccadilly Circus and have their photographs taken to send back to their families. They wanted to show them that they were now at the "centre of things" and "making history".

However, some people felt disappointed about the difference between how they had imagined life in Britain and the reality of it. People arriving in Britain desperately needed somewhere to live and were often forced into accepting appalling living conditions. This is because the only places they could find, afford or be "allowed" to live in were dirty or infested with rats. Some tenants were even charged twice as much rent as a British person for the same place.

Expensive accommodation and limited job opportunities meant that some homesick travellers may have felt trapped in Britain. The cost of a ticket back to the Caribbean became something few could afford. If determined to return, people would have to save up for months, if not years, to afford the journey. For many people who felt stranded in Britain, a small suitcase known as a "grip" became a treasured possession, as it was filled with keepsakes and memories from home and the family they may have left behind.

"Barrel children"

Children whose parents came to Britain from the West Indies in the 1940s, 50s and 60s were not always able to go with them due to the high price of travel. Parents would promise their children that they would soon be sent for and, while they waited in the Caribbean, most children went to live with grandparents or other relatives.

Many parents felt very sad about leaving their children behind, especially because they knew that it might be several years before they could earn enough money to bring them to Britain. At the time, it was not easy to make a phone call to the Caribbean, so some parents would keep in touch with their children by sending letters, parcels and barrels. These barrels were large containers filled with children's clothes, toys and food. Those children waiting to join their parents overseas became known as "barrel children" because of the barrels that held their treasures.

It could be difficult for parents and children when they were finally reunited. If children were very young when their parents left, they did not always remember them or feel comfortable being with them. Sometimes, barrel children would have new brothers and sisters who they did not know. Although they had eagerly waited to be sent for – looking up at the planes, or across the sea at the ships coming into dock – once they arrived in Britain, many children missed their grandparents and the lives they knew before.

A return journey?

Most of the people from the Caribbean islands who came to Britain came with the plan to work, save money and then return to the West Indies. However, as time passed and people settled in, plans of returning would start to fade. Often, once their children were in school and they had jobs and homes, the idea of going back to the West Indies seemed either impossible or impractical.

The Jamaican saying "while the grass is growing, the horse is starving" means that if you concentrate too hard on saving for the future and do not spend any money on enjoying yourself, your quality of life will suffer. West Indians living in Britain began to take pride in decorating their houses so they felt like they had somewhere to call home. They would often take special care to decorate their front rooms, as these became a place to welcome friends and hold "blues parties", where they played rhythm and blues and reggae music.

Most children at the time were not allowed to play in the front room because their parents wanted to keep it looking its best for visitors. They often collected special things to put in display cabinets in their front rooms, such as their smart plates, glasses and glass animals. The sofa would usually be covered in plastic to protect it from dirt, and there might be a "Blue Spot" radiogram for playing music, a plastic, pineapple-shaped ice bucket and a trolley for drinks.

The Notting Hill riots

Between the end of the Second World War (in 1945) and 1958, around 125,000 people from the Caribbean had arrived in Britain. Despite many being forced to live in difficult conditions and experiencing racial discrimination, there was still very little protection offered to them by the British government. This apparent acceptance of racism within society allowed certain groups of people to get bolder in the way they treated Black people.

One group – known as "Teddy Boys" – began to get a reputation for committing violent acts against people who were different from them. In the summer of 1958, fights were started by Teddy Boys in the streets of Notting Hill, an area of west London. Fuelled by racist hatred, groups of Teddy Boys would chase and attack any West Indian men they saw.

But, from this violence, some unity was found. West Indians who until now had thought of themselves as belonging to a particular Caribbean island, realized that, to some British people, they were all seen as the same. They decided to come together to defend themselves. The Trinidadians, who lived in Notting Hill, would often be joined by Jamaican men, who had travelled from Brixton to offer help and protection. Racial tensions and violence ran high, but when Kelso Cochrane, a young Black man from Antigua, was murdered in 1959, people of all ethnicities were shocked and knew that something had to change.

The Bristol Bus Boycott

Although London Transport had set up offices in the West Indies specifically to recruit West Indian workers, other bus companies in British towns and cities were not as welcoming. In fact, some would deliberately avoid hiring Black people. The Bristol Omnibus Company said that this was because white passengers would not want to be driven by Black people, or even sit near them. They also said that white people who already worked on the buses might leave their jobs if they had to work with Black people.

Young West Indian people, especially those of Caribbean heritage who had been born in Britain, started to fight against the prejudice they faced, rather than accept it as part of life. Inspired by reports of the freedom marches of North America and stories of how Black Americans were protesting against discrimination, Black people in Britain began to feel that they could come together in the same way.

In 1963, Black people living in Bristol publicly said that they would stop using the bus services that were run by a company who would not give Black people jobs. Many white people then joined the boycott of the Bristol Omnibus Company, and after a few months the business had lost a lot of money. Less than a year later, it was announced that the company would allow Black people to be bus drivers and conductors. It was a victory for all those who felt that people should all be treated fairly, no matter what colour their skin.

Carnival!

After the shock of the repeated violence and continuous public discrimination of Black people, West Indians living in Notting Hill felt sad and afraid. In response, some decided to try to create a happier story for themselves and their families. Remembering the joy of Carnival parades back in the Caribbean when they were children, a group of local people began to make plans to recreate Carnival on the streets of London.

The first outdoor Notting Hill Carnival was held in August 1966, and it was soon followed by Carnivals in Leeds and other British cities. It not only helped people to feel less alone and less homesick, but it also appealed to people of all ages and ethnicities – everyone was welcome at Carnival!

In the West Indian Carnival, people would dress up in costumes and masks, play steel pans and sing soca and calypso songs. It was an opportunity to put aside differences and party together as people. There were marching bands and prizes for the children with the best costumes.

Carnival would end with the crowning of a Carnival King and Queen, who, in the minds of the West Indian party-goers, were just as powerful as the British monarch – at least for one day of the year. Notting Hill Carnival is still held today and has become a diverse, community-led event of celebration and one of the world's largest street parties.

The Race Relations Acts

After fifteen years of West Indian people enduring racial discrimination and poor treatment, the pressure on the British government to act and make things better began to take effect. Some British politicians decided to change the law.

In 1965, a Race Relations Act was introduced, making it illegal to discriminate against people because of the colour of their skin, their race or ethnicity. The new law protected people in public places, such as cafés, swimming pools or cinemas, and on modes of transport, such as buses, planes and trains. In 1968, a second law was added that meant landlords could no longer turn people away because of their skin colour, race or ethnicity, and employers could not refuse to give people jobs for the same reason.

Although there were now new legal protections, Black people began to face a new wave of discrimination. The politician Enoch Powell began to publicly argue against the new Race Relations Acts, and he was supported by racist people who made signs and graffiti saying "Keep Britain white". In 1968, Powell made his famous "Rivers of Blood" speech, in which he threatened that there would be violence and blood on the streets of Britain unless Caribbean people were sent back to the West Indies. He lost his job because of the speech, but more than a hundred thousand white people sent him letters to say they agreed with him. It felt like the laws were not enough to stop the voices of hate.

The Windrush Scandal

Nearly 70 years after HMT *Empire Windrush* landed at Tilbury Docks, the name "Windrush" was back in the headlines. In 2017, journalists and activists began to uncover a story that became known as the "Windrush Scandal".

In 2012, the British government created a new rule that required everyone to provide documentation to prove they were allowed to work and claim healthcare in Britain. This caused problems for some of the people who had arrived from the Caribbean between the years 1948 and 1973.

Many of these people had never had a passport: they had come to Britain as a child on a parent's passport and so had no documentation. It was also discovered that, in 2010, the Home Office had destroyed landing cards and other official records of people's arrival in Britain, making it impossible for some to prove their legal arrival into the country. As a result, people from the Caribbean or with Caribbean heritage were denied access to healthcare, were falsely arrested and were even deported to the West Indies as "illegal immigrants".

The reports in 2017 shamed the British government into action. Some of the people who had been sent to the West Indies were allowed to come home to Britain. They were offered money because they had lost their jobs and homes, but most of them are still waiting for it and many of those affected are still fighting to prove their British citizenship.

Celebrating West Indian culture

West Indian culture has had a huge impact on what it means to be British. You can hear its influence in the music of reggae, rap and grime, and in the way that people speak in the streets. You can taste it in the food, such as jerk chicken, plantain, ackee and salt fish. You can see it in the joyful way people celebrate when the West Indies, the national cricket team of the Caribbean, are playing.

Many people living in Britain are now petitioning to remove the statues of enslavers in towns and cities. They remind people of the violence and greed of British enslavers, and it is difficult to understand why the oppressors of so many people, including the ancestors of British citizens, are still celebrated in such a way. New statues are planned to show the important contribution many cultures have made to the fabric of British society, including the Caribbean community. One of these statues was unveiled in 2022 and now stands at London Waterloo railway station, a place where so many travellers first arrived in London to start their new lives.

West Indian people and British-born people of Caribbean heritage have contributed to British culture and helped to transform Britain forever. Windrush Day, now held on 22 June every year, is a great moment to remember the sacrifices people made to rebuild Britain after the wars. It is important to remember that there is more to the West Indian communities of Britain than the image of one ship.

A Ladybird Book

collectable books for curious kids

☐ 9780241544174

☐ 9780241544167

☐ 9780241544181

☐ 9780241544198

Collect them all!

Animal Habitats
9780241416860

Baby Animals
A Ladybird Book
☐ 9780241416907

Insects and Minibeasts
A Ladybird Book
☐ 9780241417034

Sea Creatures
A Ladybird Book
☐ 9780241417072

Trees
A Ladybird Book
☐ 9780241417218

Electricity
A Ladybird Book
9780241416945

The Human Body
A Ladybird Book
☐ 9780241416983

The Solar System
A Ladybird Book
☐ 9780241417133

Trains
A Ladybird Book
☐ 9780241417171

Weather
A Ladybird Book
☐ 9780241417362

Climate Change
A Ladybird Book
9780241545669

Mountains
A Ladybird Book
☐ 9780241554975

Planet Earth
A Ladybird Book
☐ 9780241554999

Rainforests
A Ladybird Book
☐ 9780241555019

Rivers
A Ladybird Book
☐ 9780241555033

Volcanoes
A Ladybird Book
9780241555057

What to Look For in Spring
A Ladybird Book
☐ 9780241416181

What to Look For in Summer
A Ladybird Book
☐ 9780241416204

What to Look For in Autumn
A Ladybird Book
☐ 9780241416167

What to Look For in Winter
A Ladybird Book
☐ 9780241416228